ECCLES
SONG OF SONGS

Living Word BIBLE STUDIES

Joshua: All God's Good Promises
Psalms: Songs along the Way
Proverbs: The Ways of Wisdom
Ecclesiastes and Song of Songs: Wisdom's Searching and Finding
Colossians and Philemon: Continue to Live in Him
1 & 2 Thessalonians: Living the Gospel to the End

ECCLESIASTES AND SONG OF SONGS

Wisdom's Searching and Finding

KATHLEEN BUSWELL NIELSON

PUBLISHING

P.O. BOX 817 • PHILLIPSBURG • NEW JERSEY 08865-0817

ISBN: 978-1-59638-149-0

CONTENTS

Foreword by Philip Graham Ryken   vii
A Personal Word from Kathleen   xi
General Introduction   xiii
Introduction to the Poetry   xv
Introduction to Ecclesiastes   xix

LESSON 1 (ECCL. 1)
Who, What, and How?   1

LESSON 2 (ECCL. 2)
Two Tests and Two Responses   19

LESSON 3 (ECCL. 3)
Trying to Get the Big Perspective   35

LESSON 4 (ECCL. 4–5)
Holding On to the Big Perspective   49

LESSON 5 (ECCL. 6:1–8:9)
What Is Good in Life, and Where Shall We Look to Find It?   67

LESSON 6 (ECCL. 8:10–9:6)
Conclusions Coming into View   81

CONTENTS

LESSON 7 (ECCL. 9:7–10:20)
How Then Shall We Live?   97

LESSON 8 (ECCL. 11–12)
Living in Light of God   111

LESSON 9 (SONG OF SONGS, PART 1)
Encountering the Song   129
(Including the Introduction to Song of Songs)

LESSON 10 (SONG OF SONGS, PART 2)
Where There Is Love, There Is . . .   145

Notes for Leaders   163
Outline of Ecclesiastes   169
Outline of Song of Songs   171
Suggested Memory Passages   173
Notes on Translations and Study Helps   175

FOREWORD

Ecclesiastes and Song of Songs are two of the most beautiful books in the entire Bible. They are also two of the most difficult books, which explains why medieval scholars commonly identified them as the Bible's "two most dangerous books."

These books are connected to one another by more than a sense of danger, however. Although Ecclesiastes is for skeptics, and the Song of Songs is for lovers, both books are attributed to the same author: Solomon, in all his wisdom. As we read these books, therefore, as part of our ongoing quest for love and meaning in life, we receive royal wisdom from one of the world's most famous kings.

Ecclesiastes and Song of Songs also share certain literary features. Both books contain a good deal of poetry. This makes Kathleen Nielson an ideal guide for studying them, since as a literary scholar she is sensitive to the beauty of language and rich imagery of biblical poetry.

Both books are also complex in their literary structure. Although they both tell a story—of an intellectual pilgrimage in the case of Ecclesiastes, and of a romance in the Song of Songs—they do not always tell that story chronologically. Instead, they give us a collection of episodes, often followed by a thoughtful reflection or emotional response. Ecclesiastes can seem especially disorganized, for despite its overall narrative structure, it is not just a story, but also an anthology of wise writings on the vanity and futility of life.

Both of these books also give us some unique interpretive challenges. Here Dr. Nielson is to be commended for getting things exactly right, making judicious decisions about disputed matters. With regard to authorship, she correctly shows the connections to Solomon as the Bible's own way of presenting these books, without trying to claim more for Solomon than the books do themselves.

When it comes to Ecclesiastes, Dr. Nielson is careful to show how the author's negative perspective on life is balanced by passages that affirm the pleasures of eating, drinking, and working as gifts from a gracious God. This positive viewpoint is present throughout the book and not just at the end, as some scholars have argued. The result of her interpretation is a balanced view that gets the maximum spiritual benefit from Ecclesiastes.

A major issue for the Song of Songs is whether the book should be read literally or allegorically, as a love story about Christ and his church. Dr. Nielson rightly begins by taking the romance literally, helping us see what the book says at the level of a human relationship. But she also opens up new spiritual dimensions by seeing its love story in the larger context of marriage, which for the believer is always a reminder of our relationship to Christ and the love story of our own salvation—the romance of redemption.

Both Ecclesiastes and Song of Songs are important books to master in developing a Christian worldview. They deal with everyday matters such as work, food, and romance in a world that is frustrated by sin but at the same time animated by the love of God.

In its own unique way, each book draws us into a closer relationship with our Creator. Ecclesiastes teaches us to "fear God and keep his commandments, for this is the whole duty of man" (Eccl. 12:13). Song of Songs invites us into a deeper intimacy with the Son of God as both our lover and our friend (Song 5:16). My prayer, therefore, is that the Holy Spirit will use both of these books to help you grow in reverence and affection for God.

Philip Graham Ryken

A PERSONAL WORD
FROM KATHLEEN

I began to write these Bible studies for the women in my own church group at College Church in Wheaton, Illinois. Under the leadership of Kent and Barbara Hughes, the church and that Bible study aimed to proclaim without fail the good news of the Word of God. What a joy, in that study and in many since, to see lives changed by the work of the Word, by the Spirit, for the glory of Christ.

In our Bible study group, we were looking for curriculum that would lead us into the meat of the Word and teach us how to take it in, whole Bible books at a time—the way they are given to us in Scripture. Finally, one of our leaders said, "Kathleen— how about if you just write it!" And so began one of the most joyful projects of my life: the writing of studies intended to help unleash the Word of God in people's lives. The writing began during a busy stage of my life—with three lively young boys and always a couple of college English courses to teach—but through that stage and every busy one since, a serious attention to studying the Bible has helped keep me focused, growing, and alive in the deepest ways. The Word of God will do that. If there's life and power in these studies, it is simply the life and power of the Scriptures to which they point. It is ultimately the life and power of the Savior who shines through all the Scriptures from beginning to end. How we need this life, in the midst of every busy and non-busy stage of our lives!

I don't think it is just the English teacher in me that leads me to this conclusion about our basic problem in Bible study these days: we've forgotten how to *read*! We're so used to fast food that we think we should be able to drive by the Scriptures periodically and pick up some easily digestible truths that someone else has wrapped up neatly for us. We've disowned that process of careful reading . . . observing the words . . . seeing the shape of a book and a passage . . . asking questions that take us into the text rather than away from it . . . digging into the Word and letting it speak! Through such a process, guided by the Spirit, the Word of God truly feeds our souls. Here's my prayer: that, by means of these studies, people would be further enabled to read the Scriptures profitably and thereby find life and nourishment in them, as we are each meant to do.

In all the busy stages of life and writing, I have been continually surrounded by pastors, teachers, and family who encourage and help me in this work, and for that I am grateful. The most wonderful guidance and encouragement come from my husband, Niel, whom I thank and for whom I thank God daily.

May God use these studies to lift up Christ and his Word, for his glory!

GENERAL INTRODUCTION

Welcome to a study of two beautiful Old Testament books. This study will treat the books separately, although at the start we should acknowledge their connections. Both Ecclesiastes and the Song of Songs find their place in the third section of the Hebrew Bible, the "Kethubim" or "Writings." Within that section, both books form part of the "Five Scrolls," which include the Song of Songs, Ruth, Lamentations, Ecclesiastes, and Esther. All five of these books have been favorites of the Jewish people for centuries, read regularly and publicly at the major Hebrew festivals. Song of Songs was read at Passover, the most important Hebrew festival (celebrating the Jews' deliverance from Egypt). Ecclesiastes was read at the Feast of Tabernacles, the harvest festival during which the Jews traditionally spent a week in temporary shelters or "booths" to remember their time of wandering in the wilderness.

Another commonality relates to the tradition of wisdom literature, of which Ecclesiastes certainly and the Song of Songs arguably constitute a part. Wisdom literature, written not just by Jewish people but by many peoples of the ancient world, is distinguished by its philosophical approach to questions about the meaning of life. For example, the book of Job asks the deep, hard questions about suffering. The book of Proverbs asks the more practical questions about how we should live and why.

The book of Ecclesiastes is like Job in its deep questions about existence, but it also in parts resembles Proverbs in its practical observations about everyday life. Scholars have argued that the Song of Songs can rightly join the wisdom literature, as it deals with questions concerning the nature of love.

Both Ecclesiastes and the Song of Songs have traditionally been attributed to King Solomon, but the authorship of both books has in recent generations been the subject of dispute. Each study will address this question, but certainly we cannot fail to note the common textual references to this king of Jerusalem, who is presented in both books as seeking something worthy and lasting amid all the pomp and splendor of human wealth and royalty. Whoever wrote these books at the least resembles the Solomon of Proverbs who understood the power of words—poetic words in particular. Song of Songs in its entirety and Ecclesiastes in alternating sections offer particularly beautiful examples of Hebrew poetry. A basic introduction to this poetry is included in a separate introductory section and is intended to help make the study of this poetry more clear, profitable, and enjoyable.

Through these books, both part of God's inspired Word, we not only peer back into the life of the kingdom long ago; we also peer deep into eternal truths for every member of Christ's kingdom now. May the Lord bless our study of these two Old Testament treasures.

Introduction to the Poetry

Poetry speaks to us as whole people, appealing in unique ways to our imaginations and emotions as well as to our intellects. Song of Songs is one long love poem or series of poems. In Ecclesiastes, sections of poetry alternate with sections of prose. If God inspired so much poetry in these books (and indeed throughout the Scriptures), then it must be important and good for us to take in the poetic form with understanding and enjoyment.

When we read Old Testament poetry, we are reading lines originally written in the Hebrew language. Hebrew poetry's central characteristic is its balancing of "lines" (or units of thought) in a structure often called *parallelism*. What a blessing that this characteristic, in God's providence, can be communicated in translation—unlike such characteristics as rhythm and rhyme. The nature of Hebrew poetry makes it crucial to use a translation that presents the poetry in discernible lines. Most often, two (or sometimes three) parallel lines balance together to create meaning. There are three generally accepted kinds of parallelism:

1. In *synonymous parallelism*, the second line basically repeats the idea of the first line, in different words (and usually adding new shades of meaning):

> I am a rose of Sharon,
>> a lily of the valleys. (Song 2:1)

> Through sloth the roof sinks in,
>> and through indolence the house leaks. (Eccl. 10:18)

The verses from Ecclesiastes 10 offer examples of poetic proverbs, parallel lines which present practical wisdom in a poetic nutshell.

2. In *antithetic parallelism*, the second line presents a contrasting idea:

> The words of a wise man's mouth win him favor,
>> but the lips of a fool consume him. (Eccl. 10:12)

3. In *synthetic parallelism*, the second line continues or adds to the meaning of the first:

> As an apple tree among the trees of the forest,
>> so is my beloved among the young men. (Song 2:3)

> Cast your bread upon the waters,
>> for you will find it after many days. (Eccl. 11:1)

The other outstanding characteristic of Hebrew poetry (and of most poetry) is its *imagery*, or pictures. We should watch for these pictures, try to *see* them, muse over them, and relish them. For example, what happens through the verses above when we picture the beloved as a rose or a lily—or when we picture her lover as "an apple tree among the trees of the forest"? What do we grasp through the picture of casting bread upon the water? How will we connect the picture of the sun rising and setting and rising again to the sense of vanity and meaninglessness that the writer of Ecclesiastes feels? All of Scripture asks us to take in pictures: pictures of shepherds, water, light and dark, bread, paths, and on and on.

We will do well to watch the words carefully in these books, as in all of the books whose words are breathed out by God through the writers he used.

Introduction to Ecclesiastes

Ecclesiastes is a book about trying to make sense of this quickly passing, unpredictable, unfair life on earth. It is a book for questioners of all kinds. It is a book for skeptics. It is an honest book. In some ways, it is a shocking book to find in Scripture. What are we supposed to do with this cry of "Vanity of vanities. . . . All is vanity!"? People do not often say such things in the context of a community of faith.

People do say such things on their way to faith. The book of Ecclesiastes is not a bleak, repetitive cry of just one despairing note. It is more like a two-part invention, with higher and lower voices pulling back and forth until the resolution at the end. Ecclesiastes vividly portrays two perspectives: the "under the sun" perspective does not admit God into the picture, and the other perspective lines up everything in relation to one sovereign Creator God. Some scholars conclude that the book was originally written by an unbelieving writer, and that another, God-fearing writer later tried to help by adding some more positive sections about God and the goodness of life.

However, I hope you will find that a careful journey through the text reveals something closer to this: a work of art communicated in the voice of one man who introduces himself at the beginning, who tells all about his battle between these two perspectives as he tried to make sense of the world, and who ends up offering his clear conclusion that following God is the only way to go. He shapes his journey in the tradition of wisdom literature composed by many "wise men" throughout the ancient world (see the General Introduction). Such literature had a dark, contemplative side, as in the book of Job, and it also included a strain of lighter, practical wisdom, as in the book of Proverbs. Ecclesiastes, in asking its basic questions about the meaning of life, incorporates both aspects, combining some of the darker, weightier questions with a sometimes more reflective, practical tone and content.

Who is this wisdom writer? Verse 1 of chapter 1 points clearly to Solomon, who was "the son of David, king in Jerusalem"—and who was also, of course, known for his wisdom. Various questions (such as why he did not name himself as he did in Proverbs) have led some scholars to dispute Solomon's authorship and to offer various theories about later writers taking on the person and voice of Solomon. Many trustworthy thinkers today still take the text's plain pointing to Solomon at face value. Whether the writer was Solomon or someone taking on Solomon's persona, clearly he wanted to speak in some larger way than simply in his own named voice, and so he called himself Qoheleth (translated "Preacher" or "Convener" or "Teacher"). The title makes sense. Perhaps more than any other book in Scripture, this book deals with and speaks to a large, universal audience: a generic, unspecified "Preacher" would therefore be appropriate. And yet, as study of the book will show, the specifics of Solomon's life emerge clearly. It is true that no historical passages enlighten us concerning Solomon's repentance, after many years of turning his heart away from the Lord (see Lesson Five). It is an educated guess, but it is certainly not hard to imagine that he came back to the God he had known and loved so well, and that the Lord's anointed

xx

was graciously recalled in the end. The voice of the Preacher in Ecclesiastes has known much, tried much, and seen much; he has been sobered by the reality of coming death; such a voice would fit a repentant Solomon toward the end of his life. Of one thing we can be sure: that God through his Spirit inspired this writer—that these words are, as Ecclesiastes 12:11 puts it, "given by one Shepherd." The Lord God is the Shepherd who guided the writer of Ecclesiastes to grapple so honestly with the struggles of time and eternity. In this study, I have simply called the writer of Ecclesiastes what he called himself, so as to avoid controversy and also to hear the text as the writer himself intended it to be heard.

In Ecclesiastes, the plain meaning of many passages does not always jump right out! It is not a simple book. It is made up of a progression of perspectives and pictures, and it winds around in circles, in a literary tradition that sometimes seems alien to a logical, Western mind. Often the pattern of the words and pictures is crucial to the meaning. As you come across key words and phrases in the course of the study, it may be helpful to mark them in your Bible to make the patterns more visible. A group of "under the sun" phrases or a few clustered mentions of God may indicate a certain perspective emerging or reemerging. Key themes will appear in relation to the different perspectives: fear and joy, for example, regularly emerge in relation to God, but injustice, foolish words, and futile labor continually frustrate everyone under the sun.

The final message of the book is to "fear God and keep his commandments." The world of Ecclesiastes includes God, commandments, vows and sacrifices at a temple, consciousness of sin and judgment—all the most basic elements of the Israelites' community of faith. But the struggle of the speaker is a basic one: coming to acknowledge the existence and the rule of God. It is God (Elohim) who appears here—never the more personal, covenant-making LORD (Yahweh). Ecclesiastes portrays the initial steps and struggles of faith, which grow into knowing the Lord, and ultimately into knowing Jesus Christ.

The Preacher in Ecclesiastes does not know the name of Jesus. And yet, to the eye of one who knows that name, Jesus Christ is the beginning and the end of the Preacher's search. He is the Wisdom from above the sun, which reveals all earthly wisdom to be futile and foolish. He is the Creator, the Judge, the Shepherd toward whom the Preacher is drawn. He is the bread and wine the Preacher celebrates, the giver of the white robe he wears, and the very substance of the Word he receives. To take in this book as part of the Bible's whole story of redemption makes it even more lovely, as the basic melodies echo with all sorts of overtones and harmonies in the air around them.

May the words of the wise be like goads to us, their collected sayings like nails firmly fixed—given by one Shepherd.

Lesson 1 (Eccl. 1)

WHO, WHAT, AND HOW?

Chapter 1 of Ecclesiastes offers a brilliant introduction to the whole book. Who is the speaker? What is the problem? What is the method of solving it? These three questions not only set forth the scope of the book but also draw us into the book's process of questioning. We feel the intensity of the Preacher's search, and we identify with it, because he is asking our own most fundamental questions about how to make sense of what we see and experience in our brief span of time on earth.

DAY ONE—WHO IS THE SPEAKER?

To begin, read through the first chapter of Ecclesiastes. What are your first impressions of this speaker?

We first meet the speaker as "the Preacher" in Ecclesiastes 1:1. Some translations just call him "Qoheleth"—the actual Hebrew word, meaning "one who assembles or calls together." In fact, our title "Ecclesiastes" comes from the Greek translation of "Qoheleth." This title for the speaker appears three times in Ecclesiastes 1, once in the middle of the book (7:27), and three times at the end.

1. What do we learn of this Preacher in Ecclesiastes 12:9–10?

2. What else do we learn of the Preacher in Ecclesiastes 1:1 and 1:12?

3. How do the following verses relate Solomon to the one named Qoheleth?

- 1 Kings 2:10–12

- 1 Kings 4:29–34

- 1 Kings 8:1–2, 5, 14, 22, 65–66

4a. Note that the Preacher, in the book's first and final lines, is introduced in the third person ("he"). But in the main body of the book, beginning in Ecclesiastes 1:12, how does the Preacher refer to himself?

b. How might this narrative perspective affect the book and our reading of it?

DAY TWO—WHAT IS THE PROBLEM?

1. What general observations would you make about the book's opening prologue/poem in Ecclesiastes 1:2–11?

For reflection: The Preacher states the main problem of the book in the sudden, dramatic cry of Ecclesiastes 1:2. Look briefly to Ecclesiastes 12:8 to see that he will unify the book by returning to this ringing cry at the book's end; only then will he provide the proper solution to the problem of the book.

2. The Hebrew word for "vanity" is *hebel*, which connotes something unsubstantial or fleeting—like a breath or a vapor. ("Vanity of vanities" is a Hebrew superlative, implying not just much, or more, but the *most* vanity possible.) This word *hebel* occurs thirty-six times in the book. Look through just the first two chapters: How many repetitions of this word do you find? Comments?

3a. The Greek version of *hebel* appears in Romans 8:20, translated into English as "futility" or "frustration." Many believe that this is the only New Testament reference or allusion to Ecclesiastes. In Romans 8:20–21, what do you learn about this futility?

5

b. According to Genesis 3:17–19, when and why was the creation subjected to futility in this way?

.

c. According to the same verses in Genesis (3:17–19), to what is Adam made subject at this point?

4. Now read Ecclesiastes 1:3, and in the context of these other verses, comment on the Preacher's frustration.

5. Do you relate to the frustration expressed in Ecclesiastes 1:2–3? In what situations have you experienced or witnessed similar feelings?

6. From what viewpoint is the speaker looking at human toil? Page through the book and look for repeated occurrences of the last three words of Ecclesiastes 1:3. (They occur twenty-nine times in all.) Write down some thoughts concerning the perspective revealed by these words.

DAY THREE—ELABORATING ON THE PROBLEM

What does the world look like through the eyes of a fallen man—searching under the sun, trying to find meaning in a fallen world?

1. In Ecclesiastes 1:4, what aspect of human life stands out in contrast to the earth itself?

2. When the Preacher looks into the world of nature (vv. 5–7), *what* aspect of that world emerges, and *how*, through the three particular examples he chooses?

3. Think on the lines of Ecclesiastes 1:8. How is it a response to the three preceding verses?

4. In Ecclesiastes 1:9–11, how does he answer the question he asked in Ecclesiastes 1:3?

5. In what sense is the Preacher right to say that "there is nothing new under the sun"?

DAY FOUR—WHAT METHOD
WILL THE PREACHER USE?

The Preacher has poured out the problem in the poetic prologue: life is fleeting and meaningless. Now he introduces his
method of exploring this problem.

1. Ecclesiastes 1:12–18 summarize his method in two brief
   cycles, which will be more fully developed in Ecclesiastes 2. How do the two cycles (Eccl. 1:12–15 and 16–18)
   conclude similarly in their final two verses?

2. In the first cycle (vv. 12–15), what specific things does
   the Preacher want us to know about his search?

3. The book first mentions God ("Elohim": the sovereign, Creator God) in Ecclesiastes 1:13. What is the initial perspective on God here?

4. The end of Ecclesiastes 1:13 reads most literally: "What a burdensome toil God has laid on the sons of the man," or, on the sons of "Adam." How might the more literal translation enlarge our perspective on this verse?

5. How do the two pictures in the proverb of Ecclesiastes 1:15 appropriately sum up this little section?

6. In the second cycle (vv. 16–18), what is the method and focus of the search?

7. Find all the references to "wisdom" in Ecclesiastes 1:12–18. From this context, what can we say about wisdom?

8. How do the following verses enlarge our understanding of wisdom?

   • Proverbs 9:10

- Jeremiah 8:9

- Daniel 2:27–28

- 1 Corinthians 1:18–25

DAY FIVE—PONDERING THIS SEARCH

1. What do the repeated pictures of the wind in Ecclesiastes 1 make you see, feel, and understand?

2. In the context of the whole of Ecclesiastes 1, of what sort of vexation and sorrow does its final proverb (Eccl. 1:18) speak? How have you perhaps experienced or witnessed this kind of vexation and sorrow?

3. Many people regard Ecclesiastes as incredibly relevant to our modern culture. Just from your reading of Ecclesiastes 1, in what ways do you find this to be true?

4. Which verses of Ecclesiastes 1 strike you most personally, and why?

5. We've seen that Ecclesiastes already points our thoughts back to Genesis and the stark reality of a fallen world cut off from God. In conclusion, take a peek ahead and meditate for a few minutes on the very end of the story, in Revelation 21:1–5. What perspective do these verses bring to Ecclesiastes 1?

Notes for Lesson 1

Lesson 2 (Eccl. 2)

TWO TESTS AND
TWO RESPONSES

Ecclesiastes 2 expands on Ecclesiastes 1's summary of the Preacher's search for meaning. (Review the two cycles: Ecclesiastes 1:12–15 and 16–18.) When two different tests to find meaning come up with the same result, he steps back and lays out two possible responses. We can take the tests along with the Preacher, and we can choose our response.

DAY ONE—WE ALWAYS START BY DOING!

In Ecclesiastes 2:1–11, the first test, of *doing*, takes three forms:

1a. First, there is *pleasure* (Eccl. 2:1–3). What sorts of pleasure are mentioned in these verses?

b. How does 1 Kings 4:20–28 expand our perspective on these pleasures?

c. Watch TV or listen to non-Christian radio for about ten minutes. What evidence do you find that the same search for pleasure continues today?

d. How does Ecclesiastes 2:1–3 show us the Preacher's conclusions and perspectives concerning such pleasure?

2a. Second, there are *projects* (Eccl. 2:4–6). List the projects that occupied the Preacher.

b. Consider some projects you have undertaken that were perhaps similar. What have been the most satisfying and *un*satisfying aspects of these projects?

   c. How do the following verses expand our perspective
       on Solomon's projects?

       • I Kings 6:38

       • I Kings 7:1–12

       • I Kings 9:23–24, 26

3a. Third, there are *possessions* (Eccl. 2:7–8). List and evaluate
    the possessions mentioned in these verses.

b.   Read 1 Kings 10:14–29. What details strike you as you
     read this vivid description of Solomon's wealth?

Day Two—Look What I Have Done

1. The greatness mentioned in Ecclesiastes 2:9 is clearly judged
    according to the accomplishments of the previous verses.
    List all the first-person pronouns and the accompanying
    verbs in Ecclesiastes 2:4–9 ("I made," "I built," etc.).

2. What do you observe as you evaluate this list? For example,
    how do people still use this sort of list today to judge
    greatness? When and where have you used it—or had
    it used on you?

3. As you look at the first nine verses of Ecclesiastes 2, what do you think the Preacher means in verse 3 and verse 9 when he claims that his wisdom "remained with him" throughout this search?

4. It is certainly because his wisdom "remained with him" that he could finally get to the summary results of all this doing. In Ecclesiastes 2:10, how does he sum up and evaluate his experience of pleasure?

5. What do you notice about his conclusion in Ecclesiastes 2:11, as he stands back and evaluates all these activities?

6. Looking at Ecclesiastes 2:11 along with the opening verses of the whole book, what do you notice?

DAY THREE—WHEN DOING FAILS, TRY THINKING

According to Ecclesiastes 2:12, nobody coming after him could ever *do* any more than King Solomon has done, and so he turns to the second test: *thinking* about wisdom (Eccl. 2:12–16).

1. As he compares wisdom to folly, what is his *short-term judgment*, and *why* (Eccl. 2:13–14a)?

2. What is his *long-term judgment*, and *why* (Eccl. 2:14b–16)?

3. This passage brings the first of many confrontations with death, which stops all short-term arguments. Comment on the one particular aspect of his mortality that really bothers the Preacher in Ecclesiastes 2:18–19, 21.

Doing failed to construct meaning. Thinking failed to create meaning. Now the Preacher responds:

4. In Ecclesiastes 2:17–23, the Preacher summarizes his first response to the meaninglessness he finds under the sun. What words and phrases in these verses reveal his attitude and emotions?

5. Have you ever met the person sketched out for us by these words and phrases? Where? Briefly comment.

6. Looking through Ecclesiastes 2:12–23 once more, list the key words and phrases with which you are becoming familiar. Summarize the "under the sun" perspective.

DAY FOUR—ANOTHER RESPONSE BREAKS THROUGH

Another perspective consistently challenges the perspective of despair in Ecclesiastes. In the final three verses of Ecclesiastes 2, another viewpoint emerges, one not limited to "under the sun." Another possible response to unanswerable questions begins to emerge.

1. Which words or phrases in Ecclesiastes 2:24–26 reveal a different set of attitudes and emotions?

2. The reality of God clearly breaks through here. What is the role of God in each of these verses:

- Ecclesiastes 2:24

- Ecclesiastes 2:25

- Ecclesiastes 2:26

3. Looking under the sun, we saw wise people and foolish people. From the perspective above the sun, we might say, what two categories of people emerge (v. 26)?

This is only the beginning sketch of that relationship with God, which transforms despair into satisfaction and even joy. Ecclesiastes will further fill in the picture, and the entire Bible gives all the beautiful details from beginning to end. We will look further and further as we make this journey with the Preacher.

4. However, even from this short passage (2:24–26), what can we discover to be the basic elements of a proper relationship with the one true God?

5. In the final verse of Ecclesiastes 2, what different sorts of things do we see God giving to these two kinds of people?

6. What is the effect of the final statement in Ecclesiastes 2?

DAY FIVE—REVIEWING THE TEST RESULTS

1. Looking back through Ecclesiastes 2, compare and contrast the two different perspectives at work.

2. Looking back through the first two chapters, what do you find to be the rhythm or shape of the book so far?

3. The second perspective, we saw, looked up to see people in relation to God: either sinners against God or pleasers of God. Who are *sinners*, according to the following verses?

   • Ecclesiastes 7:20

- Proverbs 20:9

- Isaiah 53:6

- Romans 3:23

4. Cut off as every person is from God by our sin, what is our only hope of moving into the category of those who please God? Before answering, read and consider Hebrews 11:6 and 13:20–21.

Ecclesiastes has already pointed us toward receiving good things as gifts from the hand of God. The greatest gift, as we shall see, is Jesus Christ, whom we must receive by faith. For final reflection and discussion, consider this: Do you view your days more as toil or as a gift received from God? How does the second perspective change your life?

Notes for Lesson 2

Lesson 3 (Eccl. 3)

TRYING TO GET THE BIG PERSPECTIVE

In the midst of futility and tension, the Preacher stops in Ecclesiastes 3 to lay out a beautiful poem and a strong assertion of a larger perspective. The tension never disappears in these verses, but God's sovereign ordering of "every matter under heaven" begins to put the tension in perspective.

DAY ONE—A TIME FOR EVERYTHING

1. Ecclesiastes 3:1 offers the thesis for the subsequent poem. What is the main idea of Ecclesiastes 3:1, and how do the words and phrases work to make it vivid? *Note: "Under heaven" and "under the sun" most likely carry similar meanings.*

2. How might the assertion of Ecclesiastes 3:1 evidence either a despairing or a hopeful view, depending on one's perspective?

3. Now carefully read Ecclesiastes 3:1–8. Write down some basic initial observations about this memorable poem.

4. In Old Testament language, pairings of opposites often express totality or comprehensiveness. Through these pairings, and through the pattern of rhythmic repetitions, how does Ecclesiastes 3:2–8 develop the initial thesis of the first verse?

5. In what ways does Ecclesiastes 3:1–8 compare and contrast with the book's prologue in Ecclesiastes 1:1–11?

DAY TWO—THE RHYTHM OF GOD'S TIME

1. Why might it seem appropriate that Ecclesiastes 3:2, with its two different beginnings and endings, comes first in the pairings of this poem?

2. How does Ecclesiastes 3:3 continue similar (but different!) descriptions of beginnings and endings?

3. Within these rhythms that we all know—of life and death, beginnings and endings—all the extremes of human experience are covered in the remaining pairs of opposites. Consider, for example, the two pairs in Ecclesiastes 3:4: What aspect of human experience do they cover, and how do they appropriately follow the preceding verses?

4. Each of the next four lines (Eccl. 3:5–6) contrasts the time of gathering something to oneself with the time of giving up something. How much of life is made up of experiencing, discerning, and accepting such "times"! Comment on some ways you have seen and/or learned this.

5. Some commentators think the "time to tear" (Eccl. 3:7) refers to the tearing of garments in order to show grief, as was the practice in ancient cultures. The "time to sew" might then refer to comfort, or to joyful as opposed to grief-filled celebrations. In any case, how do both pairs in Ecclesiastes 3:7 present two opposite human activities that require discernment, bring struggle, and take care? (See also Proverbs 10:19; 15:23.)

6. How does Ecclesiastes 3:8 beautifully pull the poem to its close? Notice both the progression and the "crisscrossed" pattern (called a "chiasm" in Hebrew poetry) of these two final pairs.

DAY THREE—GOD'S TIME IN OUR HEARTS

Like many of us, the Preacher has not completed a shift to the eternal perspective; he is still holding the heavenly and earthly perspectives in tension. Note that he initially answers the poem by asking in Ecclesiastes 3:9 the same question he was asking in Ecclesiastes 1:3. However, he is gradually exposing that question to more and more truth about God.

1. What is the role of God in Ecclesiastes 3:10–13?

2. From the first two statements of Ecclesiastes 3:11, write down the two huge, wonderful acts of God, and your thoughts as you consider them. Then think back or look back to Genesis 1; what context does it offer for these statements?

3. And yet, what creates the tension in the last part of Ecclesiastes 3:11? Do you know this tension?

4. Ecclesiastes 3:12–13 brings a refrain we have met before and will meet again. How does this refrain begin to resolve the tension in Ecclesiastes 3:11? How does this refrain differ from the starting point of Ecclesiastes 1:13–14?

5. The Preacher indeed cannot grasp the whole of God, but what specific statements can he at this point make with certainty about *what God does* (Eccl. 3:14)?

6. To *fear God*, a key idea in Ecclesiastes, involves rightly acknowledging him for who he is. What aspects of God in Ecclesiastes 3:14 (and in Eccl. 3:1–14) elicit fear of him?

7. Ecclesiastes 3:15 is difficult, but seems to be affirming that God is not bound by the limitations of time. Summarize what you find in Ecclesiastes 3:1–15 concerning time and eternity.

DAY FOUR—THE PERSPECTIVE NARROWS

1. How does Ecclesiastes 3:16 raise the tension again? How does the issue raised here persist today, in your experience?

2. In what ways does Ecclesiastes 3:17 use the wisdom of the previous verses to answer the question of Ecclesiastes 3:16?

3. Summarize the additional "under the sun" objection that arises in Ecclesiastes 3:18–21. What sole kind of evidence for human knowledge does the speaker admit in these verses?

4. After these hard questions, how would you describe the nature and the tone of the "resolution" in Ecclesiastes 3:22?

5a. Consider the perspective on humans and "beasts" in Ecclesiastes 3:18–22. In what ways do you see evidence that this perspective is alive and well today?

b. What has been said previously in this chapter that might contradict this perspective? (Peek ahead to what will be said in Ecclesiastes 12:7.)

DAY FIVE—REFLECTING

1. Ecclesiastes shows a thinker pulled by two perspectives: one based on knowledge of God, and the other based on his own experience and observations. In what ways do you personally understand this struggle?

2. The Preacher has come far enough in his thinking to understand that human life makes no sense apart from the God who made it and rules it and will judge it. What light does Hebrews 11:1–6 shed on his spiritual journey?

3. How can we resist looking ahead, to the author and finisher of our faith, who has been fully revealed to us as our Lord Jesus Christ? Has your faith come to rest in Jesus, who came at the appointed time to save us from the judgment of death that we deserve? If so, how did God order the timing of your life to bring you to that point of faith?

4. Read and meditate on the following verses, and then write down some thoughts on what it means to you that God is God over all time, eternally Lord over every moment of the past, present, and future.

   • Psalm 31:14–15

   • Acts 1:7

   • Galatians 4:4

Notes for Lesson 3

Lesson 4 (Eccl. 4–5)

HOLDING ON TO THE BIG PERSPECTIVE

The Preacher is a great observer of life around him. Here in Ecclesiastes 4 and 5, the question is: How do we put what we *see* together with what we *know*? Look through Ecclesiastes 4 and note the verses that mention the Preacher's *looking* or *seeing*.

DAY ONE—I SAW . . .

1. First, the Preacher saw that *people were oppressed* around him. In Ecclesiastes 4:1, what specific observations does he make about the oppressed?

2a. What familiar phrase do you notice both toward the beginning and at the end of this little section (Eccl. 4:1–3)? How does the perspective represented by that phrase affect the declaration in Ecclesiastes 4:2–3?

b. How have you encountered such declarations in the world around you today?

3. The Preacher saw the tears and obviously grieved over the suffering of the oppressed. Do you? Read Psalm 146:7, Isaiah 53:7–8, and Hebrews 13:3. How do these verses challenge you on this subject?

4. Second, the Preacher saw that *people are motivated by envy* (Eccl. 4:4–6). According to your experience, how accurate do you find the judgment in Ecclesiastes 4:4 that all toil and skill in work are motivated by envy?

5. The lazy, unprofitable fool in Proverbs is often pictured as folding his hands. Comment on this picture in Proverbs 6:10 and 24:30. The Preacher agrees in Ecclesiastes 4:5, but goes on to make what point in verse 6?

6. What repeated image holds this little section (Eccl. 4:4–6) together, and how?

DAY TWO—MORE SEEING, BUT WITH HOPE BREAKING THROUGH

1. The Preacher saw that people are oppressed and envious, and also that *people are never content*. List everything you know about the person described in Ecclesiastes 4:7–8. Where have you seen this person?

2. What word "sandwiches" this description in Ecclesiastes 4:7–8? What is the effect of all this repetition?

3a. Finally, the Preacher saw that *people are fickle* (Eccl. 4:13–16). What familiar words and phrases do you find in this section?

b. Summarize the two main characters and the plot of this little fable (vv. 13–16).

c. What is it that is so meaningless and futile here?

4. Observe and jot down all the ways in which the people in the four sections we've observed are cut off from other people (Eccl. 4:1–3, 4–6, 7–8, 13–16).

5. As we keep seeing the hopelessness of injustice, keeping up with the Joneses, workaholism, and fleeting fortune, we keep realizing anew our need for something other than these vain things. In the midst of these dark pictures of alienated people, a ray of hope does begin to shine. Read Ecclesiastes 4:9–12 and summarize the main idea of these verses.

6. List the benefits of a close human relationship as you find them in these verses.

   Note: The passage portrays friendship, not simply marriage—although marriage certainly offers an example of such friendship. The three strands may picture two people plus God; they may also picture the great strength of three committed friends.

7. Clearly, even "under the sun," a person with a friend will gain much more for his labor. How do the following verses further explain the value of human relationships?

   • 1 Samuel 23:16

   • Proverbs 27:9, 17

   • Hebrews 10:24–25

DAY THREE—A VERTICAL RAY OF HOPE

Day Two pointed us to a horizontal ray of hope—relationships with other people. Another relationship, this time with a divine other (the source of all relationships), comes through at the beginning of Ecclesiastes 5. But this relationship with the God of the universe cannot be a casual one.

1. List all the commands, both positive and negative, in Ecclesiastes 5:1–7.

2. What central area of danger is the Preacher clearly pointing out in a person's relationship to God? In what ways have you personally encountered this danger?

3. What is "the sacrifice of fools," according to Ecclesiastes 5:1? In your answer, consider the following verses: Ecclesiastes 5:4–6; Isaiah 29:13; Hebrews 13:15.

4. In Ecclesiastes 5:1–7, the Preacher pictures both the problem and the solution as taking place *where?* *Why,* do you think?

5. Note again that culminating command in Ecclesiastes 5:7. Why is it the final and climactic one? (See also Lesson Three, Day Three, question 6.)

6. "God is in heaven and you are on earth" (Eccl. 5:3) might not mean that God is far away. What might it mean, considering the context of the book so far? What else about God is emphasized (or reemphasized) in the immediate context of Ecclesiastes 5:1–7?

7. Clearly, humble listening to God takes priority over making promises to him. But if we do make promises, what should we consider, according to the following verses?

   • Ecclesiastes 5:4

   • Numbers 30:1–2

   • Psalm 116:14 (Note again where this takes place.)

- Matthew 5:33–37

Day Four—More Clouds: Ones You Will Recognize!

The Preacher is looking about him again. This time, what catches his vision is money, money, money! In Ecclesiastes 5:8–17, locate again those three key words that describe this perspective.

1. First, the love of money leads to *oppression*. How does this occur, according to Ecclesiastes 5: 8–9?

2. Second, the love of money leads to *dissatisfaction* (Eccl. 5:10–12). What specific sort of dissatisfaction emerges in each verse (10, 11, and 12)?

3a. Third, the love of money leads to *emptiness of life and death* (5:13–17). From the perspective of material gain, how must we answer that central question of Ecclesiastes 1:3 and 3:9?

b. In Ecclesiastes 5:13–17, what are the hard facts of death that people so often spend their lives trying to deny?

4. Look back through this day's study of the love of money and the troubles it brings. When and how have you dealt personally with some of these troubles?

5. What hints of light or release do you find in Ecclesiastes 5:8–17?

For reflection and a final word on this section, read 1 Timothy 6:6–10. For a great transition to the next section, read 1 Timothy 6:17.

DAY FIVE—"BEHOLD . . ."

1. Go back through Ecclesiastes 4 and 5 and circle the word "God" each time it appears. What do you notice?

2a. List the words that tell what God is doing each of the four times he is mentioned in Ecclesiastes 5:18–20.

b. In these same verses, list the words that tell what a *person* should do.

c. What is the relationship suggested by these two lists? Write your comments as you ponder these two lists.

3. The word *lot* appears twice in Ecclesiastes 5:18–19. See also Ecclesiastes 3:22 and Ecclesiastes 9:9 for the same word or idea. Look at these examples, also read Joshua 18:8–10, and then comment on the meaning of one's "lot" or "portion."

4. What is Ecclesiastes' (and the Bible's) point about our "lot" in life, according to the following verses?

   • Ecclesiastes 5:18–19

   • Psalm 16:5

   • Proverbs 16:33

5. How does Galatians 4:4–7 fully explain our role of receiving from God what he has to give us?

Write a simple prayer asking God to make you a joyful receiver of the full lot that he has to give you.

Notes for Lesson 4

Lesson 5 (Eccl. 6:1–8:9)

What Is Good in Life, and Where Shall We Look to Find It?

Even as he acknowledges God, the Preacher is still looking around under the sun, trying in Ecclesiastes 6–8 to see what is good. "For who knows what is good for man while he lives the few days of his vain life, which he passes like a shadow?" (Eccl. 6:12).

Day One—Not a Lot of Good Things

1a. Look back to Ecclesiastes 5:19 and recall the different aspects of God's gifts to us. Which aspect of these gifts does God not give to the man in Ecclesiastes 6:2?

    b.   How might this happen? (Who could the "stranger" be?)

    c.   How do the "bookend" comments of Ecclesiastes 6:1–2 provide effective commentary on this situation?

2. If it's not wealth, how about long life with children? Why is this not a good thing for the person in Ecclesiastes 6:3?

3. The writer draws a stark, sad comparison in Ecclesiastes 6:4–6. How are the man and the stillborn child alike? How are they different?

4. Ecclesiastes 6:7–9 gives a kind of final word on the effort to get lots of good things. (This is the last picture of chasing the wind!) How would you sum up these verses?

5. The chapter's last two verses, Ecclesiastes 6:11–12, imply the inability of human beings to figure out any lasting good— even with all their wise words, as verse 11 points out! By contrast, what is implied about God in Ecclesiastes 6:10?

6. What implications for human beings can be drawn from
   the truths about God in Ecclesiastes 6:10? See also Isaiah
   45:9–12.

7. Ecclesiastes chapter 6 works as a unit and as a stopping
   point after these first chapters. Look back now at Ecclesiastes 6: What is its shape and tone?

DAY TWO—WHAT DOES GOOD (OR AT LEAST BETTER!) LOOK LIKE?

1. Ecclesiastes 7 brings another section of poetry, here a
   collection of proverbs—wisdom in proverbial poetic
   nutshells. Proverbs often work by comparisons; list all
   the comparisons you can find in Ecclesiastes 7:1–8. What
   is the general tone here?

2a. Do you find a central idea or theme(s) in Ecclesiastes 7:1–13? Explain.

b. What connections do you find with ideas in previous chapters? That is, how is this wisdom offered in light of where we've come so far in this book?

3. Many of these proverbs in Ecclesiastes 7:1–13 are (in various ways) advising people not to contend with a sovereign God. How might you find this message in several particular proverbs in this passage?

4. Which of these proverbs speaks most personally to your own tendencies to dispute with God? Explain.

DAY THREE—LOOK UP!

1. Ecclesiastes 7:13 breaks into the proverbs, names God, and acknowledges his sovereignty. Compare and contrast this verse with the book's initial statements in Ecclesiastes 1:14–15.

2. How does acknowledging God highlight our human limitations?

   • Ecclesiastes 7:13

• Ecclesiastes 7:14

• Ecclesiastes 7:20–22

• Ecclesiastes 7:19 *and* 7:23–24!

3. How did Solomon, in his own experience, find "the wickedness of folly"? See both Ecclesiastes 7:25–26 and 1 Kings 11:1–4.

4. Ecclesiastes 7:27–28 offers not a general principle, but rather one man's experience. Why do you think he came to this conclusion?

5. What is the truth offered in Ecclesiastes 7:29? How does this verse well describe Genesis 3:1–7? (How does all this connect to Ecclesiastes 7:13 and 7:20?)

DAY FOUR—LOOKING UP TO GOD

1. Tucked away in the middle of Ecclesiastes 7, verses 15–18 work toward a hint of the resolution that has been suggested and that will emerge more clearly later. First, Ecclesiastes 7:15–17 describes (with some irony) what nonsensical human dilemma and human response?

2. Ecclesiastes 7:18 (a verse puzzling to many) seems to continue the idea of avoiding all harmful extremes. The key to the tension here comes with the verse's resolution: What is it that will finally bring one out from the harm of a twisted and unbalanced world? Look back to

Ecclesiastes 3:14 and 5:7; how was the same key solution suggested there as well?

3. We saw that Ecclesiastes 7 ends on a dark note. After all the acknowledgment of sin in that chapter, the proverb beginning Ecclesiastes 8 seems to offer a lovely ray of hope. Change is possible, the Preacher suggests: I've seen it happen in a human face. What does wisdom do to a face (8:1)? Have you ever seen this happen? When and how?

4. Before he looks again to God, the Preacher offers a bit of wisdom concerning the governmental leader ordained by God. What does he recommend as wise behavior toward the king, and why (Eccl. 8:2–4)?

5. Considering what the Preacher has said about God so
   far, in what ways might he be drawing a parallel here
   between the earthly king and the heavenly King?

6. How do the assurances in Ecclesiastes 8:5–6a immediately clash with the present realities of Ecclesiastes
   8:6b–8, which then take over this section?

7. How does Ecclesiastes 8:9 well conclude this section?

DAY FIVE—STOPPING TO CONSIDER

1. Stop and consider again the wonder of God's Word, which so honestly acknowledges the tensions and the questions of human existence. How does Ecclesiastes help us better deal not just with our own tensions and questions but also with those of others?

2. In the search for what is good, this week's passages have pointed us back to creation and the fall—*and* the need for redemption, for God to make straight what has been made crooked. How does this larger framework of "creation, fall, redemption" help put the struggles of this book into perspective? In what ways could we find help and encouragement by better understanding our lives and the lives of others as part of this huge, universal story?

3. Paul sums up this "salvation story framework" in Romans 5:12–21. This is a complex passage; read it not to answer every question and clarify every phrase, but rather to get the main idea. What is Paul's point, and how does it relate to what we are reading in Ecclesiastes?

4. Conclude by spending some moments in prayer, acknowledging the "crookedness" of our world and of ourselves, and thanking God that he has provided a way to be saved, by sending his own Son.

Notes for Lesson 5

Lesson 6 (Eccl. 8:10–9:6)

CONCLUSIONS COMING INTO VIEW

The Preacher has been on a search, caught between the despairing perspective from under the sun and the perspective that acknowledges all that is beyond—namely, God. This week's passages will not let us settle on a conclusion, but as the search comes to an end, conclusions do begin to come into view!

DAY ONE—ENDS IN VIEW

1. We ended last week's lesson with the tense collision of perspectives in Ecclesiastes 8:5–9. Verses 10–13 hold similar tension, but they move in the opposite direction: from negativity and confusion toward truth and faith. This book does not let us keep our balance! How do the harsh realities in Ecclesiastes 8:10–12a collide with the truth of 12b–13? Which wins out in this section?

2. What is the key human response mentioned three times in Ecclesiastes 8:12–13? By now, we see this crucial theme developing clearly in the book. Where have we seen it before, and how is it key to the battle of perspectives going on in Ecclesiastes?

3a. In Ecclesiastes 8:12–13, what two different ends are promised for the one who fears God and the one who does not?

b.   The glimpse into eternal life is not very clear here, not even as clear as in other Old Testament passages. However, what hints can you find, even in the paradox and difficulty of these verses, that the Preacher is not talking just about earthly life?

c.   In light of other Old Testament passages, to what do these different ends ultimately refer? (See, for example, Psalms 23:6; 49:13–15; 73:23–28.)

For reflection: How can we not look forward to the one who came so that "it will be well" for us in the end? How can we not think ahead here to the Son of God, who straightened out for us what was bent and twisted by the fall? In light of Ecclesiastes' struggles and seeking, read and ponder John 3:16–18, 36.

4. After so many passages introduced with "I saw" (as in 8:10), what words in Ecclesiastes 8:12 stand out? What do these words evidence? How have these words sustained you, perhaps, in the midst of tension and doubt?

5. Consider how the larger framework of the overarching story, with its endpiece of eternal life, makes all the difference in grappling with the tensions of this life. How could remembering (indeed, *knowing*) that "it will be well" with us in the end change your life even today or this week?

DAY TWO—ATTITUDES IN VIEW

1. Chapter 8 ends as the Preacher lowers his eyes back to the earth. Why is Ecclesiastes 8:14 especially depressing after verses 12–13? Read Ecclesiastes 8:14 out loud: How does it sound to you at this point in the book?

2a. But we don't land there! Why is Ecclesiastes 8:15 especially encouraging after verse 14? Ecclesiastes 8:15 commends an attitude which is as familiar by now in this book as the despair of verse 14. List the different elements of the Preacher's prescription for living life on this earth given in Ecclesiastes 8:15.

b. How is God acknowledged in this prescription?

    c.   How does this verse answer the question of Eccle-
siastes 6:12a?

3a. But we don't land there, either! Ecclesiastes 8:16–17
looks back on and sums up the search introduced in
Ecclesiastes 1:13. What kind of effort has the Preacher
expended in the search, according to the various phrases
of these verses?

    b.   What phrases in Ecclesiastes 8:16–17 describe what
the Preacher has observed on earth, under the sun?
Is his description completely negative? How do these
verses take us back to Ecclesiastes 3:11?

c. What assertion, made three times, represents the main conclusion that shuts down this section?

4. Some would claim that the "joy" passages must actually be ironic or negative, since this book is consistently so dark. On the other hand, some want to use the "joy" passages to make the despairing parts not really so dark. However, in this book, the Preacher presents us with two strong, battling perspectives. They do affect each other, but the tension between them is real. The real despair doesn't seem able to cancel out the real joy, and the joy doesn't seem able to trump the despair. What is the effect of such tensions as we have seen in today's verses and in the whole book of Ecclesiastes so far?

DAY THREE—THE HAND OF GOD IN VIEW

Ecclesiastes 8 has brought the search to a close. With Ecclesiastes 9, the Preacher begins his wisdom teaching in light of the whole search. He would tell us how to live rightly under the sun.

1. According to all we've read so far, what would you say the Preacher means by "all this" in Ecclesiastes 9:1? Consider how many times we have met "all" and "everything" throughout this book, from the very first verses to the ones right before this point.

2. How would you sum up the beautiful first part of the Preacher's conclusion, given in the opening sentence of Ecclesiastes 9:1?

3. Who are "the righteous and the wise"? Before you write your answer, read Ecclesiastes 7:20, Romans 1:16–17, Proverbs 2:6, and Proverbs 9:10.

4. In the context of what has been affirmed about God so far in Ecclesiastes, what does it mean to be "in the hand of God"?

5. How does the second half of Ecclesiastes 9:1 balance the first? How do the two parts of this verse appropriately conclude this book's search?

6. From an "under the sun" perspective, the concept of the hand of God is not comforting. In preparation for the next day's study, read Ecclesiastes 9:2–6 as a whole, realizing that these verses are not a commentary on life after death; they are a commentary on the stark reality of death as it appears to us from under the sun.

Write down your initial observations and thoughts.

Day Four—Death in View

1. What is the point of Ecclesiastes 9:2, and how does the verse effectively communicate it?

2. In our modern civilization, in what ways and by what means have we tried to separate ourselves from the stark reality and universality of death? What are some of the results?

3. Consider the first sentence of Ecclesiastes 9:3. In what ways does it make a huge, powerful statement? Imagine, for a moment, what it is like to think about death purely from "under the sun," as this verse does.

4. The evil of universal death is not the only evil found in Ecclesiastes 9:3. What other evil is expressed in this verse, and in what vivid, powerful terms? Why is it important that the Preacher acknowledges both of these evils?

5. To what kind of hope does Ecclesiastes 9:4 refer? How strong is this hope?

6. The last phrase of Ecclesiastes 9:6 reiterates the perspective at work here. From that perspective, how does the Preacher portray death in Ecclesiastes 9:5–6?

7. Why is it important to face the reality of death and "lay it to heart," as Ecclesiastes 7:2 says?

8. Surely the Preacher wants his readers, in facing the reality of death, to face eternal and not just temporal realities. Go back to Ecclesiastes 9:1. What does that first strong assertion do for your perspective on death?

Day Five—Dealing with These Conclusions

1. In order to initially receive the gospel of Jesus Christ, who came to save sinners and give them eternal life, how is it crucial for us to grapple with the issues Ecclesiastes grapples with; issues we have seen so vividly in this week's lesson?

2. How can we conclude this week's study without making a leap ahead at this point to ask a question like this: What is the apostle Paul's perspective on death in Philippians 1:21–24?

3. Read the slightly larger context of those verses in Philippians 1:18–26. From the perspective of faith in Jesus Christ, how do "joy" and "hope" and "labor" (all concepts with which we have dealt in Ecclesiastes) take on quite different meanings?

4. Spend some moments in prayer, both thanking God for opening up the heavens to us through his Son, and also praying for our eyes and the eyes of our friends and loved ones to be increasingly opened to see "above the sun."

Notes for Lesson 6

Lesson 7 (Eccl. 9:7–10:20)

HOW THEN SHALL WE LIVE?

DAY ONE—WITH JOY

In last week's lesson, we saw the battle of perspectives in Ecclesiastes, even as the book approaches some conclusions. We ended, in the first section of Ecclesiastes 9, with a dark perspective on death. But Ecclesiastes does not end there. Again, despair does not have the last word.

1. After that dark passage in Ecclesiastes 9:1–6, what is the effect of Ecclesiastes 9:7? List all the direct commands you find in Ecclesiastes 9:7–10. What is the general effect and point of these verses?

2. White clothing and flowing oil were reserved for celebrations. The Preacher seems to be telling us not to refuse or miss the daily joy that God means to give us. In what basic activities of life are we meant to know this joy (Eccl. 9:7–9)?

3. The tension is not fully resolved. Remember that the word *vain* or *meaningless* in Ecclesiastes means "fleeting— like a vapor." What is the Preacher remembering even in Ecclesiastes 9:9, perhaps from the chapter's first six verses?

4. Ecclesiastes 9:9–10 returns to the idea of toil and work. How are we to work at anything?

5. How does the reality of death relate to our work? Before answering, read Ecclesiastes 9:10, John 9:4, and Colossians 3:23–24.

6. Go back to Ecclesiastes 9:1. What does that first statement do for your perspective on receiving life with joy, as a child of God?

DAY TWO—WITH THE WISDOM OF HUMILITY

1. The joy and energy of Ecclesiastes 9:7–10 is not without tension, either within those verses or in the verses that follow. God gives us joy, yes! But does he always give us what we expect or think we deserve? "Again" in Ecclesiastes 9:11–12 introduces a reminder—but of what? What

99

is the main point of these verses? *Note: In Hebrew, "chance" refers to unexpected events.*

2. What do the two images in Ecclesiastes 9:12 contribute here?

3. How does the statement about "time" in Ecclesiastes 9:12 connect to other verses about time in this book?

4. This book has hammered home the idea that we must live with the wisdom of humility about our expectations of earthly events—how they will happen, and when they will inevitably end. Is such wisdom, then, passive or even worth it in the end? Read on, in Ecclesiastes 9:13–18. The wisdom

of humility shows up actively in this passage. The Preacher varies the rhythm of his book here with a fable—short and to the point. Briefly, what are this story's:

* setting?

* two main characters?

* problem?

* resolution?

* moral (with a qualification)? (This is a book of tension!)

* two final judgments (and one final, crucial qualification)?

5. Try to write your own little fable, taken from your own experience, to illustrate the need for the wisdom of humility.

DAY THREE—NOT WITH FOOLISHNESS!

Ecclesiastes 10 moves into the traditional proverbial form of wisdom literature and recommends a way of living by contrasting it with its opposite.

1. Ecclesiastes 10:1 relates directly to the verses we just read in Ecclesiastes 9. What does verse 1 seem to be saying (with that vivid picture!), and how would you relate it to the preceding verses?

2. The proverbs in Ecclesiastes 10:2–3 offer general truths about wisdom and folly. What do the pictures in these verses communicate?

3a. Ecclesiastes 10:4–7 all address what kind of a situation? *Note: In these verses, the "rich" and the "princes" probably refer to people who have training and experience in leadership.*

b. Why should we not be surprised by the "evil" laid out here, according to all we've read so far in this book?

c. What is the only recommendation at this point, in these verses?

d. What further related commentary on this subject
is offered in Ecclesiastes 10:16–17—and with what
added element of evil?

4. The following verses address wisdom and foolishness
in quite "nitty-gritty" ways! What various warnings to
the foolish might one find in Ecclesiastes 10:8–11? How
might these verses support the point made back in Ecclesiastes 2:13–14?

*For reflection: Consider what all this advice about wisdom and foolish-
ness has to do with Ecclesiastes' persistent theme of fearing God. What have
we learned about God in this book? If God has sovereignly set up the universe
according to certain rules and a certain order, will we not do well to follow that
order and submit to those rules as best we can, even when we cannot fully grasp
the meaning or end of it all?*

DAY FOUR—WITH WISDOM

1a. The proverbs continue, pointing the way toward wisdom as opposed to folly. Certain themes regularly emerge in such proverbs. For example, what wise observations concerning our *words* do you find in Ecclesiastes 10:12–14 and 10:20?

b. Have you had any personal experience with the weighty consequences of words described in these verses? Briefly explain.

c. The book of Proverbs speaks much about words. Consider, for example, Proverbs 15:2, 7, 23, 28. What similar or different themes do you notice?

2a. What other warning to fools do you find in Ecclesiastes 10:15 and 10:18? (Verse 19 may join this group as a kind of ironic warning about sloth—what do you think?)

b. Recall previous comments in Ecclesiastes concerning work and toil (for example, Eccl. 2:18–23; 3:12–13; 4:4–6; 9:9–10). How do the different perspectives battling throughout this book connect with "foolish" or "wise" approaches to toil?

c. How have you seen your big-picture perspective on life affect your attitude toward your daily work?

3. Look back over Ecclesiastes 10, especially in light of this whole book we're studying. How would you offer summary "nutshells" of the Preacher's words concerning the fool and the wise person?

Day Five—Reflecting in Light of It All

Reflect a bit on the ways of living recommended to us by the wise Preacher. For each one, look up the suggested passage and consider the ways in which Jesus Christ both showed us and offers us this kind of life. Let us examine all of this in light of the full revelation of God to us. Let us live:

- with joy (see John 15:9–11; 1 Peter 1:8–9)

- with the wisdom of humility (see James 4:13–16; 1 Peter 5:6–7)

- without being fools! (see Eph. 5:15–21)

- with wisdom (see Col. 2:2–3)

Notes for Lesson 7

Lesson 8 (Eccl. 11–12)

LIVING IN LIGHT OF GOD

Throughout this book, the Preacher has held in tension the two perspectives of "under the sun" and "above the sun." We all know this struggle to figure out how God fits in with the visible life around us. In Ecclesiastes, as in the course of our lives, God breaks through and demands that we take notice. The reality of God intrudes regularly and increasingly; by the end of the book, the Preacher is not able to figure out the logical problem of God, but he is able to begin to say what it means to live rightly in relation to him. He takes what he has seen under the sun and connects it to God.

DAY ONE—LIVING IN LIGHT OF GOD THE MAKER

1a. In Ecclesiastes 11:1–6, the Preacher deals with the limitations of his human knowledge. Remember how, at the start, he devoted himself to studying and exploring this meaningless life? What has he learned about his ability to control and explain things, according to the following passages?

- Ecclesiastes 11:2

- Ecclesiastes 11:5a

- Ecclesiastes 11:5b

- Ecclesiastes 11:6

b. Human knowledge has progressed immeasurably since the time of Ecclesiastes. How would some people today take issue with these last four verses?

c.   Understanding our limitations depends on understanding who God is. How does Ecclesiastes 11:5 help clarify such understanding?

2. One sort of response to all this might be summed up by the attitude evidenced in Ecclesiastes 11:3–4. What sort of attitude(s) do you observe in these verses?

3. How do other, better responses emerge in the following verses?

•   Ecclesiastes 11:1

    Note: "Bread" is used here in the sense of "earthly goods," even as they might be sent out in ships on a commercial venture.

- Ecclesiastes 11:2

- Ecclesiastes 11:6

4. How would you generally describe the life of someone who lives out those good responses we just observed (Eccl. 11:1, 2, 6)?

5. How do the people in the following passages offer examples of throwing oneself with abandon into the hands of God?

- Daniel 3:16–18

- 2 Corinthians 8:1–5

- Philippians 2:17–18

6. Some risks are unwise and foolish to take, some are not. How would the previous verses (and the whole biblical context) help us to discern the difference?

Day Two—Living in Light of God the Judge

Ecclesiastes 11:7–10 reminds us to abandon ourselves in another way—to joy. Enjoying God's good gifts has been a consistent theme. *Don't miss joy,* this book says!

1. First, read through Ecclesiastes 11:7–10. What strikes you initially?

2. How and where can we find joy, according to Ecclesiastes 11:7 and 11:9?

3. Ecclesiastes 11:8 and 9 both offer a call to rejoice, but both qualify that call with a "but." Consider first the "but" in verse 8. What is the tension that challenges joy in this verse?

   Note: The "days of darkness" most likely describe the "evil days" of Ecclesiastes 12:1, at the close of life, described vividly in the next chapter. It is no wonder that this verse ends with that well-known "vanity" (or "breath" or "vapor"). How fast life moves to its close!

4. Ecclesiastes 11:9 has a bigger and more far-reaching "but." What is the tension that challenges joy in this verse?

For reflection: We have seen God as the Maker of all things, and now God as judge of all things—God at the beginning and God at the end. Our little world under the sun is lit up from both sides by the one eternal God.

5. The final verse of this passage certainly has a dark side that tempers the whole call to joy. What are the positive and the negative sides of the two commands in Ecclesiastes 11:10? *Note: The second phrase could be translated, "Put away evil from your flesh."*

DAY THREE—REMEMBERING YOUR CREATOR

The final chapter will move again from God as Creator to God as Judge – lighting up our existence from both ends. Hear that first clear, ringing command: "Remember also your Creator in the days of your youth" (Eccl. 12:1). Actually, many of us doing this study may qualify as "youth," in that we've perhaps not yet encountered all the troubles described in Ecclesiastes 12. So, for all of us, *now*, while we are able, let us remember our Creator.

1. First, summarize Ecclesiastes 12:1.

2. What is involved in *remembering* God, in the following passages?

    •   Deuteronomy 8:11–18

    •   Jonah 2:7–9

3. Now we get to take in this long, winding description of those "evil days"!

    This is the last, most desolate look at the end of living "under the sun." In Ecclesiastes 12:2–5, what pictures do you see? What phrases stand out? What sorts of attitudes and views of the end do these pictures and phrases evoke? Some have found pictures here of eyesight failing, or hair turning gray, or losing one's teeth. What do you think?

4. List the six different ways death is described in Ecclesiastes 12:6–7; what does each make you think of? What is the cumulative effect of this piling on of pictures?

5a. How does Ecclesiastes 12:8 complete the beautiful shape of the book? (Find the corresponding initial verse.)

    b.   How has your understanding of this cry evolved through the book?

DAY FOUR—THE BOOK'S CONCLUSIONS

This day's work is a bit lengthy, but it is crucial and it moves along quickly!

    1.   Just as Ecclesiastes began with a prologue, so it ends with an epilogue. In what ways are these two sections similar to each other and different from the main body of the book? (See Ecclesiastes 1:1–11 and 12:9–14.)

2. In Ecclesiastes 12:9–10, what do we learn about the following:

    • the Preacher

    • his method

    • the substance of the book

3. In what ways has this book indeed consisted of knowledge, words of delight, and words of truth?

4. What two pictures are we given for these wise words (12:11)? For each, explain what you think the Preacher might be telling us about the words of this book. *Note: "Goads" are wooden rods with iron spikes used to prod oxen ahead.*

   1.)

   2.)

5. The third phrase in Ecclesiastes 12:11 is striking. To whom, in the context of Scripture, does this seem to refer? (See Gen. 48:15; Pss. 23:1; 80:1–3; Ezek. 34:31.)

What a glorious God we have: Maker from the beginning, Judge at the end, and Shepherd all the way through.

6. Ecclesiastes 12:11 expresses well both the origin and the power of Scripture. What similar claims do the following verses make for the Word of God?

- 2 Timothy 3:16–17

- 2 Peter 1:20–21

- Hebrews 4:12

7. Why is the warning in Ecclesiastes 12:12a so crucial? (See also Proverbs 30:5–6 and Revelation 22:18–19.)

8. When have you most felt the truth of Ecclesiastes 12:12b? Why is this here?

9. The kinds of questions asked in Ecclesiastes are still being asked by many today, over and over again. Why is it not popular these days to give a clear answer, as the Preacher goes on to do in the final verses?

10a. Read Ecclesiastes 12:13 slowly and carefully. This final command is the culmination of a fundamental and persistent theme of the book. (See Ecclesiastes 3:14; 5:7; 7:18; 8:12–13.) Considering the content and struggle of Ecclesiastes, how is the fear of God its necessary resolution—the inevitable "end of the matter" in this book?

b. The last clause of Ecclesiastes 12:13 is literally "for this is the whole of man." This conclusion gets at the heart of everything a person is meant to be. How do you respond?

11. How does the final verse offer an appropriate concluding warning?

For reflection: Meditate for a bit on this command to fear God and keep his commandments, especially in light of his final judgment. Use the following verses to help you focus and pray: Deuteronomy 10:12–13; Psalm 33:6–11; Proverbs 8:13; Hebrews 9:27; Revelation 14:6–7.

DAY FIVE—LIVING IN THE LIGHT OF JESUS

1. The Bible, Old Testament and New, is the completed revelation of the wise words given by one Shepherd. We must interpret each part according to the whole. The Bible's whole story, from beginning to end, is about God redeeming a people for himself through Jesus Christ. Therefore, we must see Ecclesiastes always and finally in this light. How do the following verses show Christ to be the Creator, the final Judge, and the Shepherd to whom Ecclesiastes ultimately points?

   - Creator (see John 1:1–3 and Col. 1:15–16)

   - Judge (see John 5:26–27 and 2 Cor. 5:10)

   - Shepherd (see Ezek. 34:20–24 and John 10:14–15)

2a. According to 1 Peter 2:24–25, why did the good Shepherd
 lay down his life for the sheep?

  b.   According to 1 Peter 1:8–9, what do Christ's follow-
 ers *do*, and what do they *receive*?

Write a final prayer asking God to enable you to fear him,
obey him, and receive with all your heart the Son he has sent to
accomplish your salvation.

Notes for Lesson 8

Lesson 9 (Song of Songs, Part 1)

ENCOUNTERING THE SONG

Before beginning this lesson, be sure to read or review the introductory materials at the beginning of this study book. The specific introduction to Song of Songs is part of this lesson.

DAY ONE—STARTING WITH THE WORDS

What a privilege it is to study one of the most beautiful books in all of inspired Scripture! The general introductory materials present the background of the Hebrew text, the wisdom literature tradition, and the nature of Hebrew poetry. The title in the Hebrew text is "Solomon's Song of Songs," which has been variously translated as "Song of Solomon" or "Song of Songs." Before we delve into further introductory discussion, on this first day begin with *one initial reading* of the entire book. Do not read commentaries or notes—just the text! It shouldn't take too long; the eight chapters are relatively short, and your goal will be to get a general sense, not to make a detailed analysis. Try to find a block of time in which you can complete the reading, and keep on reading even when you come to words and passages that puzzle or especially interest you—we'll come back to them! Joyful reading!

DAY TWO—INTRODUCTION

On this day, please read the following introduction to the book. Mark any spots you would like to discuss or consider further.

We don't read the Song of Songs too often these days. Throughout history, it has been read often and held in special honor by God's people. Ancient Jews revered the book, calling it sublime, reading it faithfully on the eighth day of every Passover, that first and greatest of all the annual feasts. God's people compared Proverbs to the outer court of the temple, Ecclesiastes to the Holy Place, and Song of Songs to the Holy of Holies—the temple's inner sanctum of God's holy presence.

Song of Songs is indeed a personal book, which is perhaps why we tend to shy away from it. It is all about love of the most intimate kind, the love of a man and a woman—and specifically the love between a husband and a wife. Surely it should not surprise us that God devotes one book in his Word to the goodness of the way he created us as sexual beings, made to live and love within the bonds of marriage. In the very beginning, God blessed the union of the man and the woman he had made; they were a part of all that he declared "very good" (see Gen. 1:26–31). The creation of human beings as male and female surely constitutes a vital part of the divine image in which we were made. Only with sin came the shame and the perversion which distort what God originally made to be pure, holy, and reflective of his own nature. God clearly wants us to remember the ideal of married love as we encounter it in the Song of Songs: that this ideal exists according to his divine purposes, that it is joyful and celebratory, and that it is a treasure to be protected.

What a radical perspective this is, in light of our culture's growing distortion and rejection of this ideal.

Such comments take the Song of Songs literally, as an affirmation of human love as God intended it to be. For many centuries, the book was not read at all literally. Instead, it was read as an allegory, that is, as a symbolic picture of deeper, spiritual truth. The spiritual truth in the Song of Songs was taken to be the love of God for his people Israel, and further, the love of Christ for his church. In the allegorical handling of the book, the literal level was largely ignored.

We will begin on the literal level and try, first, to take Song of Songs as plainly as possible. However, any book of the Bible deepens in significance as it is connected to the larger story of the whole of Scripture. Song of Songs is not mentioned explicitly anywhere else in Scripture. But marriage is—starting in Genesis, as we have seen, and then stretching out all the way through the book of Revelation. What is the meaning of marriage in the Bible? As we shall see in our study, marriage in both Old and New Testaments is given to us as a picture of God's love for his people. When we read the Song of Songs, we should not only be elevated in our understanding of the ideal of human love, but we should also be spurred on in our love for God, who loves us so amazingly in Christ Jesus. We are all ultimately made for that bridegroom. G. Campbell Morgan puts it well, in his *Analyzed Bible* (Revell, 1964, p. 197):

> The songs should be treated, then, first as simple and yet sublime songs of human affection. When they are thus understood, reverently the thoughts may be lifted into the higher value of setting forth the joys of the communion between the spirit of man and the Spirit of God, and ultimately between the Church and Christ.

A few other introductory matters must be discussed. Some commentators see three rather than two main characters in the

Song of Songs: not just Solomon and the maiden, but Solomon, the maiden, and a shepherd whom she truly loves. In this view, a corrupt Solomon is trying to divert the maiden's love from her rustic lover to himself. Scenes of royalty and court life are taken to stand in contrast to scenes in the country, with sheep, gardens, and vineyards. The interpretive problem is knotty, because the original texts list no characters and do not divide up or allocate the various lyrics in any way.

The more traditional view, with two main characters, understands the pastoral scenes to be part of the whole poetic structure of the Song, in which (as in love poetry of many different cultures and centuries) the lovers are often described using images of nature. The maiden of the story does indeed come from a rustic setting, with actual vineyards and flocks, and Solomon, as the story seems to tell it, may indeed venture into this country setting to find her. But it is important to notice that the poetry pictures the woman in terms of a garden herself, with choice fruits to be enjoyed. The lover is pictured in terms of an apple tree, a young stag—and perhaps a rustic shepherd.

We will assume the more traditional and, I think, the plainer meaning of the text. One can certainly build a good case for the "love triangle theory," but to do that seems to require more guessing and more stretching of the text than to accept the two characters clearly identified: Solomon and the Shulammite maiden.

Part of the reason that the more modern theory evolved, it seems, is a reluctance to accept King Solomon as a worthy lover in such a love poem as Song of Songs. Such reluctance comes less from the text of the book itself than from readers' own wonderings. For example, how could such a magnificent testament to married love between one man and one woman be authored by (as has been traditionally claimed), or even just in honor of, a man who had seven hundred wives and three hundred concubines (1 Kings 11:1–8)? Must we not affirm, however, that God in his providence could have brought Solomon to an understanding and an articulation of greater truths than he had been able consistently to live out? Surely the Spirit of God did that for every writer of inspired Scripture. King Solomon—a splendid, wise ruler of God's people, one to whom the nations of the world streamed—points us to the Lord not only through his splendor but also through his failure: an even greater ruler than Solomon was needed. Just so, this book points us not only to the wonder of human love, but also, especially when human love fails us, to the even greater wonder of God's love.

Another part of the reason various dramatic theories have emerged is that readers have attempted to identify a chronological or even just a logical shape to the progression of poems in Song of Songs, from beginning to end. They have tried to squeeze the work into the shape of a modern drama, with some sort of plot development. Even just a glimpse into the background of Hebrew literature helps here. Hebrew stories and poetry, throughout the Old Testament and elsewhere, often follow what is called a "chiastic" structure. This simply means that the work has a central pivot of meaning, from which it moves outwards symmetrically in both directions. The beginning and the ending, then, will match, in a sense, as they are both farthest away from the middle. A chiasmus is not sequential or logical in the way one might expect; it is circular, full of crossings, like a flower with petals growing out from the beautiful center. The increasingly acknowledged chiastic form of Song of Songs celebrates marriage at its center, in the wedding and consummation celebrated in Song of Songs 3:6–5:1. On both sides of this center point, as we shall see, are placed what are most likely dream scenes, full of the fears and longings of lovers approaching such a grand union (Song 3:1–5; 5:2–8). The book's earlier section may generally reflect the initial stages of attraction and "falling in love," while the later section includes a final affirmation to conclude the book. Seeing this structure at work in the Song of Songs allows us to read the poetry as an organic and coherent series of love songs, rather than a dramatic sequence to be fit into our own logical molds. It also puts the central focus of the work where it belongs: on the celebration of marriage between a man and a woman.

We will do well from the start to aim to take in the beauty of the words—the poetry. The various voices in this poetry wind the celebration of love into a beautiful, lyrical pattern. We should relish the rich imagery, enjoy the rhythm of the parallel poetic lines, and experience with the speakers the full range of love's joy, yearnings, pleasures, doubts, and unyielding strength. "Many waters cannot quench love, neither can floods drown it" (Song 8:7). What an affirmation there in the final chapter! How that second line, with its synonymous parallelism, not only repeats the meaning but also immensely deepens it! May we come away from the Song of Songs not only having relished the poetry but also having grasped that kind of love.

DAY THREE—WHAT AND WHO

1a. The title in the original has two parts: "Song of Songs" and "of Solomon." Consider the first part: "Song of Songs." What similar wordings do you find in Deuteronomy 10:17 and Ecclesiastes 1:2?

b. How, then, would you explain the meaning of this first part of the title? (Use 1 Kings 4:32 in your answer.)

2. The second part of the title, "of Solomon," could be translated "by Solomon" or "about Solomon" or "for Solomon." From this verse and from the whole text, many conclude that Solomon wrote this book. Jot down any details you learn about Solomon in these verses of this book:

    •   Song of Songs 3:6–11

    •   Song of Songs 8:11–12

3. Just from the first chapter, what can we learn about the central female character?

4a. What can you observe in the following verses about the group of people who participate in these poems?

- Song of Songs 1:4

- Song of Songs 3:5

- Song of Songs 3:10–11

- Song of Songs 6:1

b. What guesses or observations might you make about this group? (Psalm 45:14 offers a possibility; we'll come back to this psalm.)

Day Four—Listening In

1. The first two chapters let us meet and listen to the two lovers before we read of the marriage celebration in Song of Songs 3. This is a great opportunity to begin to appreciate the imagery that fills and colors the book. As you examine the lovers' words about and to each other in the following verses, write down the pictures or comparisons (metaphors or similes) you find, and for at least several of them, react with a few comments:

    •   Song of Songs 1:2

    •   Song of Songs 1:3

- Song of Songs 1:5

- Song of Songs 1:9

- Song of Songs 1:13–14

- Song of Songs 1:15

- Song of Songs 2:1

- Song of Songs 2:2

- Song of Songs 2:3

- Song of Songs 2:9

- Song of Songs 2:14

2a. What *attitudes* do you notice in these lovers?

- Song of Songs 1:4

- Song of Songs 1:6

- Song of Songs 1:7

- Song of Songs 2:3–6

- Song of Songs 2:10–13

- Song of Songs 2:16

b. Comment on this list of attitudes as a whole.

3a. Song of Songs 2:7 is an important verse, the first occur-rence of a refrain that is repeated throughout the book. Look also at Song of Songs 3:5 and 8:4. The tone is obviously serious and commanding ("I adjure you" or "I charge you"). The speaker's identity is uncertain, although in each case the refrain seems to continue whose words? (And in each case, what is the general subject or situation immediately preceding the refrain?)

b. What is this charge about, and why is it crucial enough to be repeated throughout this love poetry?

c. Consider to whom the charge is addressed. How does this seem appropriate?

DAY FIVE—REFLECTING

1. Consider, on this last day, some of the possible implications and applications of what we've taken in so far. First, how do you react to the love you glimpse in this book?

2. In what ways is it good for us to see this kind of love portrayed so openly in the Bible?

3. How does the Bible consistently affirm marriage between a man and a woman as good? Consider Matthew 19:1–6, John 2:1–11, and Hebrews 13:4.

4. What is the most striking verse or thought you've found so far in the Song of Songs? Comment a bit.

5. In what ways might this book be especially helpful and appropriate for our society today?

Notes for Lesson 9

Lesson 10 (Song of Songs, Part 2)

WHERE THERE IS LOVE, THERE IS . . .

What a full portrait of love is given us in the Song of Songs! Having introduced ourselves to the main elements of the book in Lesson Nine, let us probe more deeply in this lesson by looking at five different aspects of love that emerge clearly through further study.

DAY ONE—WHERE THERE IS LOVE, THERE IS FEARFULNESS

Human love does often involve certain kinds of fear at certain points. Two passages in particular communicate honestly and hauntingly this sometimes fearful aspect of love. These passages appear on either side of the central marriage celebration of the book, causing that center to shine ever more brightly in contrast to the shadowy dreams before and after it.

1. One passage begins in Song of Songs 3:1; the other begins in Song of Songs 5:2. How are the situations and settings of these two passages similar?

2a. In Song of Songs 3:1–5, what is the nature of the maiden's fear?

   b. How does the maiden refer to her beloved? (How many times?)

   c. How do the details of the setting seem especially appropriate?

   d.   How does this probable dream resolve in Song of
        Songs 3:4–5?

3a. In the second passage (Song 5:2–8, probably a dream
     as well), the plot thickens. What, specifically, does the
     maiden fear here (perhaps several things)?

   b.   What do you think is the saddest verse in the second
        dream, and why?

   c.   Note and comment on the difference in the reso-
        lution here (5:6–8), as opposed to that of the first
        dream (3:4–5).

4. In what ways do you identify, or do you think many people can identify, with the fears of these dreams?

DAY TWO—WHERE THERE IS LOVE, THERE IS MARRIAGE

I know; that's not always true. But in this story, and in God's scheme, love and marriage do go together. The book's central, pivotal marriage celebration comes in Song of Songs 3:6–5:1. In Solomon's time, betrothal (the engagement agreement) came before the marriage celebration and was almost as binding as marriage itself—with the same commitment to faithfulness. When the day of the actual wedding finally arrived, the ceremony included a large procession of the bridegroom with his friends to the bride's house, where the bride and her attendants would be waiting. The finest possible linens and jewels were to be worn. The bridegroom would then escort his bride (along with all the friends) back to his house for the wedding supper—a great celebration with many people and much singing and feasting. The evening ended with prayers and blessings, after which the couple was escorted to the nuptial chamber. The wedding festivities often continued for a week or so, with continued feasting and partying.

1. What elements of the marriage ceremony do you see:

   • perhaps even in Song of Songs 1:4 (a glimpse of the climax in the poem's opening)?

   • in Song of Songs 3:6–11?

   • in Song of Songs 4:16–5:1?

2. Consider the broader biblical perspective on marriage suggested by the following passages. In each, briefly, how does marriage picture for us a larger spiritual truth? (In the three Old Testament references, God is speaking to his people Israel; the three New Testament references deal with the relationship of Christ to the church.)

   • Isaiah 54:5–6

- Jeremiah 2:1–3

- Hosea 2:16–20

- 2 Corinthians 11:1–2

- Ephesians 5:23–25

- Revelation 19:7–9

3a. One other reference helps us make the jump from Song of Songs to this larger context. First, read quickly through Psalm 45, which is called a "wedding song" for the king. What connections do you notice with the Song of Songs?

  b. Now, read the verses from Psalm 45 quoted in Hebrews 1:8–9. This New Testament passage tells us these verses are *about whom?* Comment.

4. This spiritual dimension of marriage, centered ultimately in the love of Christ, enlarges and deepens our contemplation of the Song of Songs. Take a few moments to think back, from this perspective, on what we've studied so far. Jot down any thoughts and observations that come to mind. How does the whole

biblical context of God's love for his people affect your understanding of the love pictured in this book?

DAY THREE: WHERE THERE IS LOVE, THERE IS DECLARATION OF LOVE

1. The lover's poem in Song of Songs 4 might be called an epithalamion, or a wedding song, in which, typically, the bridegroom declares the beauty of his bride, often from head to toe! Part of loving, it seems, is having this impulse to extol the loved one in words. The husband-king is very full of words, and very thorough with them, in Song of Songs 4! The woman is certainly not simply a silent responder, however; she responds beautifully in Song of Songs 4:16, picking up on her beloved's imagery. And her similar epithalamion appears a bit later, in Song of Songs 5:10–16. Read carefully through these love songs (4:1–5:1 and 5:10–16) and pick several verses or images to write down and comment on.

   Note #1: One commentator has argued for Solomonic authorship using the writer's extensive knowledge of plant and animal life as proof! See 1 Kings 4:33.

Note #2: *Goats then and there generally had long, wavy, black hair. A large flock on a hillside makes the whole hillside look alive—like the bride's flowing dark hair, which is evidently not completely covered by her veil (Song 4:1).*

Note #3: *With regard to such verses as Song of Songs 4:4, don't take the images too literally! What might the imagery suggest? Dignity? Worthiness of such wealth of adornment?*

Note #4: *Do pick the garden as one of the images to comment on! Be sure to notice the comparison of the woman to a beautiful garden in Song of Songs 4:12—5:1. How is this garden, hidden away here at the center of the book, described? These verses bring the marriage passage to its deepest intimacy. How is the picture of the garden beautifully and appropriately used?*

2. What rich and sensuous celebration here! What can we learn from these passages about physicality and sexuality—and the pleasure to be found in them?

3. Read Song of Songs 6:1–7:10. The praise and celebration continue to flow out from the center of this book. What do you observe in these verses about the *different voices*, the *attitudes* evidenced here, and the *imagery*? Again, pick several images to comment on. Refer to specific verses in your comments.

Note: There are a number of difficult references and uncertain phrases in these verses. Tirzah, for example, in Song of Songs 6:4, was an old Canaanite city, evidently a picturesque one. "Shulammite," in Song of Songs 6:13, is a title for the woman and is either a variation of "Shunammite" (i.e., "from Shunem") or a form of Solomon's name, meaning that she belongs to him. The tower of Lebanon, in Song of Songs 7:4, perhaps suggests the white color of the limestone cliffs of Lebanon, rather than a gigantic nose!

4. What a wonderful impulse—to praise one's beloved in beautiful words! What applications might be drawn here?

5. How might this impulse to praise fit with the larger spiritual perspective? Consider, for example, Psalm 34:1–3 and 1 Peter 2:9.

DAY FOUR—WHERE THERE IS LOVE, THERE IS EXCLUSIVE GIVING OF ONESELF

1. In the midst of further lyrical declarations of love, the beloved offers several especially lovely expressions of *giving.* This book certainly offers a joint celebration and a joint giving. What is the spirit and the substance of each of the following passages?

   • Song of Songs 7:11–13

   • Song of Songs 8:1–2

   • Song of Songs 8:10–12

2. In what specific ways does Song of Songs 8 seem to take us back to Song of Songs 1?

3. It is good to remember that this book is not logically or chronologically organized (see p. 133). After we've celebrated the wife's giving of herself, we come back to the "little sister" in Song of Songs 8:8–9 (cf. Song 1:6). What do you think the brothers are saying here?

4. Think about this waited-for, exclusive giving of oneself in marriage, and then think about our society today. What do you see?

DAY FIVE—WHERE THERE IS LOVE, THERE IS . . .

1. *You* complete this sentence for the final time, using the climactic passage in Song of Songs 8:6–7 as your text from which to work. Think these verses through carefully, perhaps taking the time to memorize them. Muse on each vivid picture with which the woman here expresses her love. And then express in your own words the several beautiful aspects of love celebrated here at the end of the Song of Songs.

   Note #1: The engraved stone or metal seal was often worn on a cord around the neck and was used to mark possession or ownership; its imprint was like the personal signature of its owner.

   Note #2: There is some dispute about whether the last line of Song of Songs 8:6 should be translated as "a mighty flame" or "the very flame of the LORD." If the latter is correct, this is the only place in the Song where God's name appears. Even without the name, the image may suggest the divine kindling of a most intense flame.

2. Song of Songs might suggest this: "Where there is love there is a *community* in which it rightly thrives." What elements of this book would support this statement?

3. In what ways is the context of Christian and church community important to the love of a man and a woman in all its stages?

4. Consider the closing two verses of the book. What scene do you picture? How do these voices calling to one another in this way (and even the reference to friends) appropriately conclude the Song of Songs?

5. Page back through this beautiful book one final time. If someone asked you to sum up this book and explain its value in a nutshell, what would you say?

Notes for Lesson 10

NOTES FOR LEADERS

What a privilege it is to lead a group in studying the Word of God! Following are six principles offered to help guide you as you lead.

1. THE PRIMACY OF THE BIBLICAL TEXT

If you forget all the other principles, I encourage you to hold on to this one! The Bible is God speaking to us, through his inspired Word—living and active and sharper than a two-edged sword. As leaders, we aim to point people as effectively as possible into this Word. We can trust the Bible to do all that God intends in the lives of those studying with us.

This means that the job of a leader is to direct the conversation of a group constantly back into the text. If you "get stuck," usually the best thing to say is: "Let's go back to the text and read it again. . . ." The questions in this study aim to lead people into the text, rather than into a swirl of personal opinions about the topics of the text; therefore, depending on the questions should help. Personal opinions and experiences will often enrich your group's interactions; however, many Bible studies these days have moved almost exclusively into the realm of "What does this mean to me?" rather than first trying to get straight on "What does this mean?"

We'll never understand the text perfectly, but we can stand on one of the great principles of the Reformation: the *perspicuity* of Scripture. This simply means *understandability*. God made us word-creatures, in his image, and he gave us a Word that he wants us to understand more and more, with careful reading and study, and shared counsel and prayer.

The primacy of the text implies less of a dependence on commentaries and answer guides than often has been the case. I do not offer answers to the questions, because the answers are in the biblical text, and we desperately need to learn how to dig in and find them. When individuals articulate what they find for themselves (leaders included!), they have learned more, with each of their answers, about studying God's Word. These competencies are then transferable and applicable in every other study of the Bible. Without a set of answers, a leader will not be an "answer person," but rather a fellow searcher of the Scriptures.

Helps *are* helpful in the right place! It is good to keep at hand a Bible dictionary of some kind. The lessons themselves actually offer context and help with the questions as they are asked. A few commentaries are listed in the "Notes on Translations and Study Helps," and these can give further guidance after one has spent good time with the text itself. I place great importance as well on the help of leaders and teachers in one's church, which leads us into the second principle.

2. THE CONTEXT OF THE CHURCH

As Christians, we have a new identity: we are part of the body of Christ. According to the New Testament, that body is clearly meant to live and work in local bodies, local churches. The ideal context for Bible study is within a church body—one that is reaching out in all directions to the people around it. (Bible studies can be the best places for evangelism!) I realize that these studies will be used in all kinds of ways and places; but whatever the context, I would hope that the group leaders have a layer of solid church leaders around them, people to whom they can go with questions and concerns as they study the Scriptures. When a leader doesn't know the answer to a question that arises, it's really OK to say, "I don't know. But I'll be happy to try to find out." Then that leader can go to pastors and teachers, as well as to commentaries, to learn more.

The church context has many ramifications for Bible study. For example, when a visitor attends a study and comes to know the Lord, the visitor—and his or her family—can be plugged into the context of the church. For another example, what happens in a Bible study often can be integrated with other courses of study within the church, and even with the preaching, so that the whole body learns and grows together. This depends, of course, on the connection of those leading the study with those leading the church—a connection that I have found to be most fruitful and encouraging.

3. THE IMPORTANCE OF PLANNING AND THINKING AHEAD

How many of us have experienced the rush to get to Bible study on time . . . or have jumped in without thinking through what will happen during the precious minutes of group interaction . . . or have felt out of control as we've made our way through a quarter of the questions and used up three-quarters of the time!

It is crucial, after having worked through the lesson yourself, to think it through from the perspective of leading the discussion. How will you open the session, giving perhaps a nutshell statement of the main theme and the central goals for the day? (Each lesson offers a brief introduction that will help with the opening.) Which questions do you not want to miss discussing, and which ones could you quickly summarize or even skip? How much time would you like to allot for the different sections of the study?

If you're leading a group by yourself, you will need to prepare extra carefully—and that can be done! If you're part of a larger study, perhaps with multiple small groups, it's helpful for the various group leaders to meet together and to help each other with the planning. Often, a group of leaders meets early on the morning of a study, in order to help the others with the fruit of their study, plan the group time, and pray—which leads into the fourth principle.

4. THE CRUCIAL ROLE OF PRAYER

If these words we're studying are truly the inspired Word of God, then how much we need to ask for his Spirit's help and guidance as we study his revelation! This is a prayer found often in Scripture itself, and a prayer God evidently loves to answer: that he would give us understanding of his truth, according to his Word. I encourage you as a leader to pray before and as you work through the lesson, to encourage those in your group to do the same, to model this kind of prayer as you lead the group time, to pray for your group members by name throughout the week, and to ask one or two "prayer warriors" in your life to pray for you as you lead.

5. THE SENSITIVE ART OF LEADING

Whole manuals, of course, have been written on this subject! Actually, the four principles preceding this one may be most fundamental in cultivating your group leadership ability. Again, I encourage you to consider yourself not as a person with all the right answers, but rather as one who studies along with the people in your group—and who then facilitates the group members' discussion of all they have discovered in the Scriptures.

There is always a tension between pouring out the wisdom of all your own preparation and knowledge, on the one hand, and encouraging those in your group to relish and share all they have learned, on the other. I advise leaders to lean more heavily toward the latter, reserving the former to steer gently and wisely through a well-planned group discussion. What we're trying to accomplish is not to cement our own roles as leaders, but to participate in God's work of raising up mature Christians who know how to study and understand the Word—and who will themselves become equipped to lead.

With specific issues in group leading—such as encouraging everybody to talk, or handling one who talks too much—I encourage you to seek the counsel of one with experience in leading groups. There is no better help than the mentoring and prayerful support of a wise person who has been there! That's even better than the best "how-to" manual. If you have a number of group leaders, perhaps you will invite an experienced group leader to come and conduct a practical session on how to lead.

Remember: the default move is, "Back to the text!"

6. The Power of the Scriptures to Delight

Finally, in the midst of it all, let us not forget to delight together in the Scriptures! We should be serious but not joyless! In fact, we as leaders should model for our groups a growing and satisfying delight in the Word of God—as we notice its beauty, stop to linger over a lovely word or phrase, enjoy the poetry, appreciate the shape of a passage from beginning to end, laugh at a touch of irony or an image that hits home, wonder over a truth that pierces the soul.

May we share and spread the response of Jeremiah, who said:

Your words were found, and I ate them,
  and your words became to me a joy
  and the delight of my heart. (Jer. 15:16)

Suggested Outline of Ecclesiastes

To make a logical outline of Ecclesiastes is a formidable and perhaps impossible task. One might do better to create an abstract painting, with dark and light shades swirling around each other in all sorts of configurations. The following is offered in the most general terms and with acknowledgment of many possible variations and much ambiguity.

I. Prologue: All is vanity. (1:1–11)

II. Wisdom's observations: From under the sun, with light sometimes breaking through.
   A. The Preacher shares his experience of vanity, although he acknowledges the hand of God at work. (1:12–2:26)
   B. The Preacher both rues and affirms the mysteries of time and eternity, and the sovereign presence of God behind it all. (3:1–15)
   C. The Preacher points out the widespread wickedness of people headed only for the grave, and for the judgment of God. (3:16–22)
   D. The Preacher sees more vanity under the sun, but offers some wisdom on how to live in the midst of it. (4:1–16)

E. The Preacher commands the fear of God. (5:1–7)

F. The Preacher sees the vanity of accumulating riches, but also the joy of receiving God's good gifts. (5:8–20)

G. The Preacher qualifies that joy: God's gifts, under the sun, are not finally good or satisfying. (6:1–12)

H. The Preacher reaches for wisdom (and for God) amid the limitations of a fallen, "crooked" world. (7:1–29)

I. The Preacher more clearly points to the wisdom of fearing God and receiving his good gifts, but with consistent dark strains that relate to the evils and limitations of human existence. (8:1–17)

III. Wisdom's teaching: Reaching from under the sun toward the light of God.

A. The Preacher sums up life (and death) under the sun. (9:1–6)

B. The Preacher commands joy in the gifts of God, even in light of the reality of death. (9:7–10)

C. The Preacher commends wisdom, even though it be unrewarded and limited. (9:11–10:20)

D. The Preacher calls us to live joyfully and humbly in light of God the Creator and Judge of all, even in the face of evil and death. (11:1–12:8)

IV. Epilogue: Fear God and keep his commandments. (12:9–14)

Suggested Outline
of Song of Songs

An outline of Song of Songs? Impossible! Here is one of many impossible ways:

I. Celebrating the Discovery of Love (1:1–2:17)

  II. Dream (3:1–5)

    III. The Marriage Celebration (3:6–5:1)

  IV. Dream (5:2–8)

V. Celebrating the Discovery of Love (5:9–8:14)

SUGGESTED MEMORY PASSAGES

What gain has the worker from his toil? I have seen the business that God has given to the children of man to be busy with. He has made everything beautiful in its time. Also, he has put eternity into man's heart, yet so that he cannot find out what God has done from the beginning to the end. I perceived that there is nothing better for them than to be joyful and to do good as long as they live; also that everyone should eat and drink and take pleasure in all his toil—this is God's gift to man. I perceived that whatever God does endures forever; nothing can be added to it, nor anything taken from it. God has done it, so that people fear before him. (Eccl. 3:9–14)

Guard your steps when you go to the house of God. To draw near to listen is better than to offer the sacrifice of fools, for they do not know that they are doing evil. Be not rash with your mouth, nor let your heart be hasty to utter a word before God, for God is in heaven and you are on earth. Therefore let your words be few. For a dream comes with much business, and a fool's voice with many words. (Eccl. 5:1–3)

The end of the matter; all has been heard. Fear God and keep his commandments, for this is the whole duty of man. For God will bring every deed into judgment, with every secret thing, whether good or evil. (Eccl. 12:13–14)

> Set me as a seal upon your heart,
>   as a seal upon your arm,
> for love is strong as death,
>   jealousy is fierce as the grave.
> Its flashes are flashes of fire,
>   the very flame of the LORD.
> Many waters cannot quench love,
>   neither can floods drown it.
> If a man offered for love
>   all the wealth of his house,
>   he would be utterly despised. (Song 8:6–7)

Notes on Translations
and Study Helps

This study can be done with any reliable translation of the Bible, although I do recommend the English Standard Version for its essentially literal but beautifully readable translation of the original languages. In preparing this study, I have used and quoted from the ESV, published by Crossway Bibles in Wheaton, Illinois.

These lessons are designed to be completed with only the Bible open in front of you. The point is to grapple with the text, not with what others have said about the text. The goal is to know, increasingly, the joy and reward of digging into the Scriptures, God's breathed-out words, which are not only able to make us wise for salvation through faith in Christ Jesus but also profitable for teaching, reproof, correction, and training in righteousness, so that each of us may be competent, equipped for every good work (2 Tim. 3:15–17). To help you "dig in," basic and helpful contexts and comments are given throughout the lessons. I have used and learned from the following books in my own study and preparation; you may find sources such as these helpful at some point.

NOTES ON TRANSLATIONS AND STUDY HELPS

GENERAL HANDBOOKS:

The Crossway Comprehensive Concordance of the Holy Bible: English Standard Version. Compiled by William D. Mounce. Wheaton: Crossway Books, 2002. (Other concordances are also available, from various publishers and for different translations.)

The Illustrated Bible Dictionary. 4 vols. Wheaton: Tyndale House Publishers, 1980. (*The Zondervan Pictorial Encyclopedia of the Bible* is similarly helpful.)

Ryken, Leland, James Wilhoit, and Tremper Longman III, eds. *Dictionary of Biblical Imagery.* Downers Grove, IL: InterVarsity Press, 1998.

Ryken, Leland, Philip Ryken, and James Wilhoit. *Ryken's Bible Handbook.* Wheaton: Tyndale House Publishers, 2005.

Vine's Complete Expository Dictionary of Old and New Testament Words. Nashville: Thomas Nelson, 1984.

COMMENTARIES:

Bridges, Charles. *A Commentary on Ecclesiastes.* Carlisle, PA: Banner of Truth Trust, 1961 (first published 1860).

Carr, G. Lloyd. *The Song of Solomon: An Introduction and Commentary.* Tyndale Old Testament Commentary. Downers Grove, IL: InterVarsity Press, 1984.

Eaton, Michael A. *Ecclesiastes: An Introduction and Commentary.* Tyndale Old Testament Commentary. Downers Grove, IL: InterVarsity Press, 1983.

Garrett, Duane, and Paul R. House. *Song of Songs / Lamentations.* Word Biblical Commentary. Nashville: Thomas Nelson, 2004.

Gledhill, Tom. *The Message of the Song of Songs: The Lyrics of Love.* The Bible Speaks Today. Downers Grove, IL: InterVarsity Press, 1994.

Kaiser, Walter C., Jr. *Ecclesiastes: Total Life.* Chicago: Moody Bible Institute, 1979.

Kidner, Derek. *A Time to Mourn, and a Time to Dance.* Downers Grove, IL: InterVarsity Press, 1976.

Kidner, Derek. *The Wisdom of Proverbs, Job and Ecclesiastes.* Downers Grove, IL: InterVarsity Press, 1985.

Longman, Tremper, III. *The Book of Ecclesiastes.* New International Commentary on the Old Testament. Grand Rapids: Eerdmans, 1998.

Longman, Tremper, III. *Song of Songs.* New International Commentary on the Old Testament. Grand Rapids: Eerdmans, 2001.

Ryken, Leland. *Words of Delight: A Literary Introduction to the Bible.* Grand Rapids: Baker Book House, 1987. 2nd ed., 1993.

A native of St. Louis, Missouri, **Kathleen Nielson** holds M.A. and Ph.D. degrees in literature from Vanderbilt University and a B.A. from Wheaton College. She has taught in the English departments at Vanderbilt University, Bethel College (Minnesota), and Wheaton College. She is the author of numerous Bible studies, as well as various articles and poems. Kathleen has directed and taught women's Bible studies at several churches, speaks extensively at women's conferences and retreats, and serves on the board of directors of Focus on the Family. Kathleen is married to Dr. Niel Nielson, president of Covenant College in Lookout Mountain, Georgia. Kathleen and Niel have three sons.